MONTHLY BUDGET

MONTH

1st Income   **2nd Income**

	Budget	Amount

Total

MONTHLY BUDGET

MONTH _____

INCOME

1st Income _____   **2nd Income** _____

EXPENSES

Budget	Amount

Total

MONTHLY BUDGET

MONTH _____

INCOME

1st Income _____   **2nd Income** _____

EXPENSES

	Budget	Amount

Total

MONTHLY BUDGET

MONTH _____

INCOME

1st Income _____   **2nd Income** _____

EXPENSES

	Budget	Amount

Total

MONTHLY BUDGET

MONTH

INCOME

1st Income _____   **2nd Income** _____

EXPENSES

Budget	Amount

Total

MONTHLY BUDGET

MONTH _____

INCOME

1st Income _____   **2nd Income** _____

EXPENSES

	Budget	Amount

Total

MONTHLY BUDGET

MONTH _____

INCOME

1st Income _____   **2nd Income** _____

EXPENSES

	Budget	Amount

Total

MONTHLY BUDGET

MONTH _____

INCOME

1st Income _____   **2nd Income** _____

EXPENSES

	Budget	Amount

Total

MONTHLY BUDGET

MONTH

1st Income   2nd Income

	Budget	*Amount*

Total

MONTHLY BUDGET

MONTH _____

INCOME

1st Income _____   **2nd Income** _____

EXPENSES

	Budget	Amount

Total

MONTHLY BUDGET

MONTH

INCOME

1st Income   **2nd Income**

EXPENSES

	Budget	Amount

Total

MONTHLY BUDGET

MONTH _____

INCOME

1st Income _____   **2nd Income** _____

EXPENSES

	Budget	Amount

Total

MONTHLY BUDGET

MONTH _____

INCOME

1st Income _____ 2nd Income _____

EXPENSES

	Budget	Amount

Total

MONTHLY BUDGET

MONTH _____

INCOME

1st Income _____   **2nd Income** _____

EXPENSES

	Budget	Amount

Total

MONTHLY BUDGET

MONTH _____

INCOME

1st Income _____ **2nd Income** _____

EXPENSES

	Budget	Amount

Total

MONTHLY BUDGET

MONTH

INCOME

1st Income _____   **2nd Income** _____

EXPENSES

	Budget	Amount

Total

MONTHLY BUDGET

MONTH

INCOME

1st Income _____   **2nd Income** _____

EXPENSES

Budget	Amount

Total

MONTHLY BUDGET

MONTH _____

INCOME

1st Income _____ **2nd Income** _____

EXPENSES

	Budget	Amount

Total

MONTHLY BUDGET

MONTH _____

INCOME

1st Income _____   **2nd Income** _____

EXPENSES

Budget	Amount

Total

MONTHLY BUDGET

MONTH _____

INCOME

1st Income _____   **2nd Income** _____

EXPENSES

	Budget	Amount

Total

MONTHLY BUDGET

MONTH

INCOME

1st Income _____ **2nd Income** _____

EXPENSES

Budget	Amount

Total

MONTHLY BUDGET

MONTH _____

INCOME

1st Income _____   **2nd Income** _____

EXPENSES

	Budget	Amount

Total

MONTHLY BUDGET

MONTH _____

INCOME

1st Income _____   **2nd Income** _____

EXPENSES

	Budget	Amount

Total

MONTHLY BUDGET

MONTH _____

INCOME

1st Income _____ **2nd Income** _____

EXPENSES

	Budget	Amount

Total

MONTHLY BUDGET

MONTH

INCOME

1st Income _____ 2nd Income _____

EXPENSES

	Budget	Amount

Total

MONTHLY BUDGET

MONTH _____

INCOME

1st Income _____   **2nd Income** _____

EXPENSES

	Budget	Amount

Total

MONTHLY BUDGET

MONTH _____

INCOME

1st Income _____   **2nd Income** _____

EXPENSES

	Budget	Amount

Total

MONTHLY BUDGET

MONTH _____

INCOME

1st Income _____   **2nd Income** _____

EXPENSES

	Budget	Amount

Total

MONTHLY BUDGET

MONTH

INCOME

1st Income _____ **2nd Income** _____

EXPENSES

Budget	Amount

Total

MONTHLY BUDGET

MONTH _____

INCOME

1st Income _____ **2nd Income** _____

EXPENSES

	Budget	Amount

Total

MONTHLY BUDGET

MONTH

INCOME

1st Income _____   **2nd Income** _____

EXPENSES

	Budget	Amount

Total

MONTHLY BUDGET

MONTH _____

INCOME

1st Income _____   **2nd Income** _____

EXPENSES

	Budget	Amount

Total

MONTHLY BUDGET

MONTH _____

INCOME

1st Income _____   **2nd Income** _____

EXPENSES

	Budget	Amount

Total

MONTHLY BUDGET

MONTH _____

INCOME

1st Income _____   **2nd Income** _____

EXPENSES

	Budget	Amount

Total

MONTHLY BUDGET

MONTH _____

INCOME

1st Income _____   **2nd Income** _____

EXPENSES

Budget	Amount

Total

MONTHLY BUDGET

MONTH

INCOME

1st Income   **2nd Income**

EXPENSES

	Budget	Amount

Total

MONTHLY BUDGET

MONTH _____

1st Income _____   2nd Income _____

Budget	Amount

Total

MONTHLY BUDGET

MONTH _____

INCOME

1st Income _____ **2nd Income** _____

EXPENSES

	Budget	Amount

Total

MONTHLY BUDGET

MONTH _____

INCOME

1st Income _____ **2nd Income** _____

EXPENSES

Budget	Amount

Total

MONTHLY BUDGET

MONTH _____

INCOME

1st Income _____   **2nd Income** _____

EXPENSES

Budget	Amount

Total

MONTHLY BUDGET

MONTH

1st Income _____   **2nd Income** _____

Budget	Amount

Total

MONTHLY BUDGET

MONTH

INCOME

1st Income _____   **2nd Income** _____

EXPENSES

	Budget	Amount

Total

MONTHLY BUDGET

MONTH _____

INCOME

1st Income _____   **2nd Income** _____

EXPENSES

	Budget	Amount

Total

MONTHLY BUDGET

MONTH _____

INCOME

1st Income _____   **2nd Income** _____

EXPENSES

	Budget	Amount

Total

MONTHLY BUDGET

MONTH _____

INCOME

1st Income _____ **2nd Income** _____

EXPENSES

	Budget	Amount

Total

MONTHLY BUDGET

MONTH _____

INCOME

1st Income _____   **2nd Income** _____

EXPENSES

	Budget	Amount

Total

MONTHLY BUDGET

MONTH

INCOME

1st Income _____   **2nd Income** _____

EXPENSES

Budget	Amount

Total

MONTHLY BUDGET

MONTH

INCOME

1st Income _____   **2nd Income** _____

EXPENSES

	Budget	Amount

Total

MONTHLY BUDGET

MONTH

INCOME

1st Income _____ 2nd Income _____

EXPENSES

Budget	Amount

Total

MONTHLY BUDGET

MONTH

INCOME

1st Income _____   **2nd Income** _____

EXPENSES

	Budget	Amount

Total

MONTHLY BUDGET

MONTH _____

INCOME

1st Income _____ **2nd Income** _____

EXPENSES

Budget	Amount

Total

MONTHLY BUDGET

MONTH _____

INCOME

1st Income _____   **2nd Income** _____

EXPENSES

	Budget	Amount

Total

MONTHLY BUDGET

MONTH

INCOME

1st Income _____   **2nd Income** _____

EXPENSES

	Budget	Amount

Total

MONTHLY BUDGET

MONTH

INCOME

1st Income _____ **2nd Income** _____

EXPENSES

	Budget	Amount

Total

MONTHLY BUDGET

MONTH _____

INCOME

1st Income _____   **2nd Income** _____

EXPENSES

	Budget	Amount

Total

MONTHLY BUDGET

MONTH _____

INCOME

1st Income _____ **2nd Income** _____

EXPENSES

	Budget	Amount

Total

MONTHLY BUDGET

MONTH

INCOME

1st Income _____   2nd Income _____

EXPENSES

Budget	Amount

Total

MONTHLY BUDGET

MONTH _____

INCOME

1st Income _____ **2nd Income** _____

EXPENSES

	Budget	Amount

Total

MONTHLY BUDGET

MONTH _____

INCOME

1st Income _____   2nd Income _____

EXPENSES

	Budget	Amount

Total

MONTHLY BUDGET

MONTH _____

INCOME

1st Income _____ **2nd Income** _____

EXPENSES

Budget	Amount

Total

MONTHLY BUDGET

MONTH _____

INCOME

1st Income _____ **2nd Income** _____

EXPENSES

	Budget	Amount

Total

MONTHLY BUDGET

MONTH _____

INCOME

1st Income _____ **2nd Income** _____

EXPENSES

	Budget	Amount

Total

MONTHLY BUDGET

MONTH

INCOME

1st Income _____   **2nd Income** _____

EXPENSES

Budget	Amount

Total

MONTHLY BUDGET

MONTH _____

INCOME

1st Income _____   2nd Income _____

EXPENSES

	Budget	Amount

Total

MONTHLY BUDGET

MONTH _____

1st Income _____ **2nd Income** _____

Budget	Amount

Total

MONTHLY BUDGET

MONTH _____

INCOME

1st Income _____ **2nd Income** _____

EXPENSES

Budget	Amount

Total

MONTHLY BUDGET

MONTH _____

1st Income _____   2nd Income _____

	Budget	Amount

Total

MONTHLY BUDGET

MONTH _____

INCOME

1st Income _____   **2nd Income** _____

EXPENSES

Budget	Amount

Total

MONTHLY BUDGET

MONTH _____

INCOME

1st Income _____ **2nd Income** _____

EXPENSES

Budget	Amount

Total

MONTHLY BUDGET

MONTH

INCOME

1st Income _____   **2nd Income** _____

EXPENSES

	Budget	Amount

Total

MONTHLY BUDGET

MONTH

INCOME

1st Income _____   2nd Income _____

EXPENSES

	Budget	Amount

Total

MONTHLY BUDGET

MONTH _____

INCOME

1st Income _____ **2nd Income** _____

EXPENSES

	Budget	Amount

Total

MONTHLY BUDGET

MONTH

INCOME

1st Income _____ 2nd Income _____

EXPENSES

Budget	Amount

Total

MONTHLY BUDGET

MONTH _____

INCOME

1st Income _____   **2nd Income** _____

EXPENSES

Budget	Amount

Total

MONTHLY BUDGET

MONTH

INCOME

1st Income   2nd Income

EXPENSES

Budget	Amount

Total

MONTHLY BUDGET

MONTH _____

INCOME

1st Income _____   **2nd Income** _____

EXPENSES

Budget	Amount

Total

MONTHLY BUDGET

MONTH _____

INCOME

1st Income _____   **2nd Income** _____

EXPENSES

Budget	Amount

Total

MONTHLY BUDGET

MONTH _____

INCOME

1st Income _____   2nd Income _____

EXPENSES

	Budget	**Amount**

Total

MONTHLY BUDGET

MONTH

INCOME

1st Income .... 2nd Income ....

EXPENSES

Budget	Amount

Total

MONTHLY BUDGET

MONTH _____

INCOME

1st Income _____   **2nd Income** _____

EXPENSES

	Budget	Amount

Total

MONTHLY BUDGET

MONTH

INCOME

1st Income _____   **2nd Income** _____

EXPENSES

Budget	Amount

Total

MONTHLY BUDGET

MONTH _____

INCOME

1st Income _____   **2nd Income** _____

EXPENSES

	Budget	Amount

Total

MONTHLY BUDGET

MONTH

INCOME

1st Income _____   2nd Income _____

EXPENSES

	Budget	Amount

Total

MONTHLY BUDGET

MONTH _____

INCOME

1st Income _____   **2nd Income** _____

EXPENSES

	Budget	Amount

Total

MONTHLY BUDGET

MONTH _____

INCOME

1st Income _____ **2nd Income** _____

EXPENSES

Budget	Amount

Total

MONTHLY BUDGET

MONTH _____

INCOME

1st Income _____ **2nd Income** _____

EXPENSES

	Budget	Amount

Total

MONTHLY BUDGET

MONTH

INCOME

1st Income _____   **2nd Income** _____

EXPENSES

	Budget	*Amount*

Total

MONTHLY BUDGET

MONTH _____

INCOME

1st Income _____   **2nd Income** _____

EXPENSES

	Budget	Amount

Total

MONTHLY BUDGET

MONTH

INCOME

1st Income _____   **2nd Income** _____

EXPENSES

	Budget	Amount

Total

MONTHLY BUDGET

MONTH _____

INCOME

1st Income _____ **2nd Income** _____

EXPENSES

Budget	Amount

Total

MONTHLY BUDGET

MONTH

INCOME

1st Income _____ 2nd Income _____

EXPENSES

	Budget	Amount

Total

MONTHLY BUDGET

MONTH _____

INCOME

1st Income _____ **2nd Income** _____

EXPENSES

Budget	Amount

Total

MONTHLY BUDGET

MONTH _____

INCOME

1st Income _____ **2nd Income** _____

EXPENSES

Budget	Amount

Total

MONTHLY BUDGET

MONTH _____

INCOME

1st Income _____   **2nd Income** _____

EXPENSES

Budget	Amount

Total

MONTHLY BUDGET

MONTH _____

INCOME

1st Income _____   2nd Income _____

EXPENSES

Budget	Amount

Total

MONTHLY BUDGET

MONTH _____

INCOME

1st Income _____ **2nd Income** _____

EXPENSES

	Budget	Amount

Total

MONTHLY BUDGET

MONTH _____

INCOME

1st Income _____   **2nd Income** _____

EXPENSES

	Budget	Amount

Total

MONTHLY BUDGET

MONTH _____

INCOME

1st Income _____   **2nd Income** _____

EXPENSES

Budget	Amount

Total

MONTHLY BUDGET

MONTH

1st Income _____ **2nd Income** _____

Budget	Amount

Total

MONTHLY BUDGET

MONTH _____

INCOME

1st Income _____ **2nd Income** _____

EXPENSES

	Budget	Amount

Total

MONTHLY BUDGET

MONTH

INCOME

1st Income _____   2nd Income _____

EXPENSES

Budget	Amount

Total

MONTHLY BUDGET

MONTH _____

INCOME

1st Income _____ **2nd Income** _____

EXPENSES

	Budget	Amount

Total

MONTHLY BUDGET

MONTH _____

INCOME

1st Income _____   **2nd Income** _____

EXPENSES

	Budget	Amount

Total

MONTHLY BUDGET

MONTH _____

INCOME

1st Income _____   **2nd Income** _____

EXPENSES

	Budget	Amount

Total

MONTHLY BUDGET

MONTH

INCOME

1st Income   **2nd Income**

EXPENSES

	Budget	Amount

Total

MONTHLY BUDGET

MONTH _____

INCOME

1st Income _____   **2nd Income** _____

EXPENSES

	Budget	Amount

Total

MONTHLY BUDGET

MONTH

INCOME

1st Income   2nd Income

EXPENSES

Budget	Amount

Total

MONTHLY BUDGET

MONTH _____

INCOME

1st Income _____   **2nd Income** _____

EXPENSES

	Budget	Amount

Total

MONTHLY BUDGET

MONTH _____

INCOME

1st Income _____   **2nd Income** _____

EXPENSES

	Budget	Amount

Total

MONTHLY BUDGET

MONTH _____

INCOME

1st Income _____   **2nd Income** _____

EXPENSES

	Budget	Amount

Total

MONTHLY BUDGET

MONTH _____

1st Income _____   **2nd Income** _____

	Budget	Amount

Total

MONTHLY BUDGET

MONTH _____

INCOME

1st Income _____ **2nd Income** _____

EXPENSES

	Budget	Amount

Total

MONTHLY BUDGET

MONTH

INCOME

1st Income _____ **2nd Income** _____

EXPENSES

	Budget	Amount

Total

MONTHLY BUDGET

MONTH _____

INCOME

1st Income _____   2nd Income _____

EXPENSES

	Budget	*Amount*

Total

MONTHLY BUDGET

MONTH

INCOME

1st Income _____   **2nd Income** _____

EXPENSES

Budget	Amount

Total

MONTHLY BUDGET

MONTH _____

1st Income _____ **2nd Income** _____

	Budget	Amount

Total

MONTHLY BUDGET

MONTH

INCOME

1st Income _____   **2nd Income** _____

EXPENSES

	Budget	Amount

Total

MONTHLY BUDGET

MONTH

INCOME

1st Income _____   **2nd Income** _____

EXPENSES

	Budget	Amount

Total

MONTHLY BUDGET

MONTH

INCOME

1st Income _____   **2nd Income** _____

EXPENSES

	Budget	Amount

Total

MONTHLY BUDGET

MONTH _____

INCOME

1st Income _____   **2nd Income** _____

EXPENSES

	Budget	Amount

Total

MONTHLY BUDGET

MONTH _____

INCOME

1st Income _____ **2nd Income** _____

EXPENSES

Budget	Amount

Total

MONTHLY BUDGET

MONTH _____

INCOME

1st Income _____ **2nd Income** _____

EXPENSES

	Budget	Amount

Total

MONTHLY BUDGET

MONTH

INCOME

1st Income _____ **2nd Income** _____

EXPENSES

	Budget	Amount

Total

MONTHLY BUDGET

MONTH _____

INCOME

1st Income _____ **2nd Income** _____

EXPENSES

	Budget	Amount

Total

MONTHLY BUDGET

MONTH _____

INCOME

1st Income _____   **2nd Income** _____

EXPENSES

	Budget	Amount

Total

MONTHLY BUDGET

MONTH

INCOME

1st Income _____   **2nd Income** _____

EXPENSES

	Budget	Amount

Total

MONTHLY BUDGET

MONTH

1st Income _____   2nd Income _____

Budget	Amount

Total

MONTHLY BUDGET

MONTH _____

INCOME

1st Income _____ **2nd Income** _____

EXPENSES

	Budget	Amount

Total

MONTHLY BUDGET

MONTH _____

INCOME

1st Income _____   **2nd Income** _____

EXPENSES

Budget	Amount

Total

MONTHLY BUDGET

MONTH _____

INCOME

1st Income _____ **2nd Income** _____

EXPENSES

	Budget	Amount

Total

MONTHLY BUDGET

MONTH

INCOME

1st Income _____   2nd Income _____

EXPENSES

Budget	Amount

Total

MONTHLY BUDGET

MONTH _____

INCOME

1st Income _____   **2nd Income** _____

EXPENSES

Budget	Amount

Total

MONTHLY BUDGET

MONTH

INCOME

1st Income _____ **2nd Income** _____

EXPENSES

Budget	Amount

Total

MONTHLY BUDGET

MONTH _____

INCOME

1st Income _____   **2nd Income** _____

EXPENSES

	Budget	*Amount*

Total

MONTHLY BUDGET

MONTH

INCOME

1st Income _____ **2nd Income** _____

EXPENSES

	Budget	*Amount*

Total

MONTHLY BUDGET

MONTH _____

INCOME

1st Income _____   **2nd Income** _____

EXPENSES

Budget	Amount

Total

MONTHLY BUDGET

MONTH _____

INCOME

1st Income _____   **2nd Income** _____

EXPENSES

Budget	Amount

Total

MONTHLY BUDGET

MONTH _____

INCOME

1st Income _____   **2nd Income** _____

EXPENSES

Budget	Amount

Total

MONTHLY BUDGET

MONTH

INCOME

1st Income .... 2nd Income ....

EXPENSES

	Budget	*Amount*

Total

MONTHLY BUDGET

MONTH _____

INCOME

1st Income _____   **2nd Income** _____

EXPENSES

Budget	Amount

Total

MONTHLY BUDGET

MONTH

INCOME

1st Income _____   **2nd Income** _____

EXPENSES

	Budget	Amount

Total

MONTHLY BUDGET

MONTH _____

INCOME

1st Income _____ **2nd Income** _____

EXPENSES

	Budget	Amount

Total

MONTHLY BUDGET

MONTH _____

INCOME

1st Income _____   2nd Income _____

EXPENSES

	Budget	Amount

Total

MONTHLY BUDGET

MONTH _____

INCOME

1st Income _____   **2nd Income** _____

EXPENSES

	Budget	Amount

Total

MONTHLY BUDGET

MONTH _____

INCOME

1st Income _____   **2nd Income** _____

EXPENSES

Budget	Amount

Total

MONTHLY BUDGET

MONTH _____

INCOME

1st Income _____ **2nd Income** _____

EXPENSES

	Budget	Amount

Total

MONTHLY BUDGET

MONTH

INCOME

1st Income   2nd Income

EXPENSES

Budget	Amount

Total

MONTHLY BUDGET

MONTH _____

INCOME

1st Income _____   **2nd Income** _____

EXPENSES

	Budget	Amount

Total

MONTHLY BUDGET

MONTH

INCOME

1st Income _____   **2nd Income** _____

EXPENSES

Budget	Amount

Total

MONTHLY BUDGET

MONTH _____

INCOME

1st Income _____   **2nd Income** _____

EXPENSES

Budget	Amount

Total

MONTHLY BUDGET

MONTH _____

INCOME

1st Income _____   **2nd Income** _____

EXPENSES

	Budget	Amount

Total

MONTHLY BUDGET

MONTH

INCOME

1st Income **2nd Income**

EXPENSES

Budget	Amount

Total

MONTHLY BUDGET

MONTH _____

INCOME

1st Income _____   **2nd Income** _____

EXPENSES

Budget	Amount

Total

MONTHLY BUDGET

MONTH _____

INCOME

1st Income _____   **2nd Income** _____

EXPENSES

	Budget	Amount

Total

MONTHLY BUDGET

MONTH

INCOME

1st Income _____   **2nd Income** _____

EXPENSES

Budget	Amount

Total

MONTHLY BUDGET

MONTH _____

INCOME

1st Income _____   **2nd Income** _____

EXPENSES

	Budget	Amount

Total

MONTHLY BUDGET

MONTH _____

INCOME

1st Income _____   **2nd Income** _____

EXPENSES

	Budget	Amount

Total

MONTHLY BUDGET

MONTH _____

INCOME

1st Income _____   **2nd Income** _____

EXPENSES

Budget	Amount

Total